THE LANGUAGE OF HEART

MUFADDAL ALIASGAR
BAYADWALA

I want to dedicate this book to my parents - Farida and Aliasgar, my brother Taher and sister-in-law Fatema, and the three loves of my life - my wife Nisreen and my children Burhanuddin and Yusuf.

Contents

Preface

I like to read books a lot, no matter whether they are fiction, non-fiction, or history. but initially, I couldn't visualize how to make a career out of it.

It was in December 2011 when all my childhood friends gathered for a long time. Then, as they were returning back, I wrote a poem about them. they loved it very much. This is how the writer inside me was born.

Acknowledgements

For this book, my first and biggest thanks go to my family members - my mom Farida, dad Aliasgar, wife Nisreen, children Burhanuddin and Yusuf, brother Taher and sister-in-law Fatema. They are the ones who have always trusted me and guided me toward my passion for writing. I will always owe my success to them.

I will even thank my friend circle 'MAGIC GROUP' - Darshan Kabra, Dinesh Jain, Minal Mehta, Raunak Laddha, Alfiya Saifee, Nikita Tiwari, Sneha Mutha, Akshat Agrawal, and Taher Bayadwala. They are the ones for whom I had written my first poem. They loved it a lot and so, the writer inside me was born. Thank you MAGIC.

1. THE SOIL CRIES

Feathers loaded hard, their burdened arms and brain.
A child's heart cries, free me from this chain.
Nehru's soil always cries,
For child labour, the nation dies.
        The roses and their buds, coloured dark red.
        For ages, they saw continuous bloodshed.
        Gandhi's soil always cries,
        For violence, the nation dies.
Against the enemies, our brave men stand.
While always firmly guarding our borderland.
Netaji's soil always cries,
For invasion, the nation dies.
        Their steps have limits and aren't allowed to learn.
        Girls are made homebound and aren't allowed to earn.
        Savitri bai's soil always cries,
        For girls' illiteracy, the nation dies.
Folks always fight for the faith we create.
And adding upon that the lands we separate.
Sardar Patel's soil always cries,
For partition, the nation dies.
        For dowries and rapes, the victim is a girl.
        Folks kill her when, the oyster has a pearl.
        Rani Laxmi bai's soil always cries,

For domestic violence, the nation dies.

Bearing all the odds, the farmer sows the seed.

But the nation is always ruled by greed.

Chandrashekhar Azad's soil always cries,

For corruption, the nation dies.

To the killer terrorist, the rule serves.

After the blast which badly shook our nerves.

Bhagat Singh's soil always cries,

For terrorism, the nation dies.

For the good crown, he makes himself the king.

But for him, filing his belly is the only thing.

Mangal Panday's soil always cries,

For slavery, the nation dies.

2. THE INDIAN TASTE.

People living in India and having western foods' lust,
Someday taste the Indian taste, as for our tongue it's a must.

Filled with tomatoes and cucumber,
Sandwiches all will remember.
But the yummy taste doesn't lessen,
Of the pav – vada made of besan.

Though sandwich is not a waste,
But Pav – wada is the real taste.

When the stomach gets stricken with hunger,
We fill it with a burger.
But the best is filling our belly,
With the delicious dabeli.

Though burger is not a waste,
But dabeli is the real taste.

Everyone likes Pizza's slice,
Because to have it, it feels nice.
But the craze in us doesn't fade,
For the parathas which are homemade.

Though pizza is not a waste,
But paratha is the real taste.

Everyone goes nuts,
Hearing the name of donuts.

But becomes crazy like a baby,
On seeing the crunchy jalebi.
Though Donut is not a waste,
But jalebi is the real taste.

We always like it, as it seem,
Various flavours of ice – cream.
But our hearts gets fluffy,
On seeing the delicious kulfi.
Though ice – cream is not a waste,
But kulfi is the real taste.

It has always been fun,
The play of noodles sucking,
But the best will be always bhel,
Which makes our lips licking.
Though noodles are not a waste,
But bhel is the real taste.

In the scorching summer heat,
Soft – drinks always puts off our thirst.
But the best is our sharbat,
Which always increases our lust.
Though Soft – drinks are not a waste,
But sharbat is the real taste.

We always have a patch – up,
With our yummy tomato ketchup.
But the meal is only complete with a jar,
Filled with the home – made achaar.
Though ketchup is not a waste,

But achaar is the real taste.

People gets freeze,
On seeing the creamy pastries.
But all are ready to die,
Just to get a bite of mithai.

Though pastry is not a waste,
But mithai is the real taste.

We always walk our steps,
Towards where we get wraps.
But towards samosa we always run,
Because its taste has always been fun.

Though warp is not a waste,
But samosa is the real taste.

Western food may be tasty,
But finally it's just a food.
The real fun is the Indian taste,
Which always cheers our mood.

Though western food is not a waste,
But Indian food is the real taste.

3. VALENTINES DAY.

It's called the week of hearts,
When the world of love shines.
It's none other than love's week,
It's the week of Valentines.

The first day is on the seventh,
The day celebrated for rose.
With the best person whom,
As a life – partner we chose.

The second day is on the eight,
The best day to go on date.
To our partner we propose,
With loved filled heart and a rose.

The third day is on the ninth,
Which we celebrate with a chocolate.
The sweetest thing that we share,
With our sweet love – mate.

The fourth day is on the tenth,
Meant only for teddy bear.
With our love partner,
These soft moments we share.

The fifth day is on the eleventh,
The day to make a promise.
For a strong bond with the person,

We don't want to miss.

The sixth day is on the twelfth,
The day for love and kiss.
It's a deep feeling for both,
Which gives our hearts a bliss.

The seventh day is on the thirteenth,
The time of hugs and understanding.
It grows pure love in us,
And that love is never ending.

And finally comes the day of fourteenth,
The day when two hearts combine.
It's the day of love and joy,
It's the day of Valentine.

4. A WOMAN'S SILENT SCREAM.

Inside the mother's oyster,
When God keeps the pearl,
For the lust of a boy,
They kill the baby girl.

> Come on, let us make a choice,
> Against female foeticide, let us raise our voice.

Limits are made for her,
She is not allowed to study.
At tender age in the kitchen cage,
She is made ready.

> Come on, let us make a choice,
> Against female illiteracy, let us raise our voice.

She becomes a rape target,
When the bird desires to fly.
Her beauty attracts the beast,
And she is left alone to die.

> Come on, let us make a choice,
> Against rape, let us raise our voice.

With a bridal dress and tears in eyes,
Her feelings are always hidden.
She has to leave her house,
With shoulders under dowry burden.

> Come on, let us make a choice,
> Against dowry, let us raise our voice.

Daily at her place,
Home violence becomes a habit.
No defence and only violence,
Like wolves attacking a rabbit.

> Come on, let us make a choice,
> Against domestic violence, let us raise our voice.

As soon as her husband dies,
She is declared as a widow.
She isn't free to live her way,
As if she is a cursed shadow.

> Come on, let us make a choice,
> Against false practices against widows, let us raise our voice.

Throughout her life,
Her feelings always bleed.
But no one cares,
To listen her voiceless plead.

> Come on, let us make a choice,
> Against violence against women, let us raise our voice.

5. HISTORY OF INDIA.

Glory has always ruled,
On India – the great land.
In the name of empires,
Which stood very grand.

> The great king Dhana Nanda,
> Made his army very grand.
> On seeing his mighty strength,
> Even Alexander couldn't stand.

The great king Puru,
Even after his brutal defeat,
Ordered the mighty Alexander,
"As a king, you shall treat."

> The great king Chandragupt Maurya,
> To unify India, he had a dream.
> He stood with Chanakya's ideas,
> And made his empire supreme.

The great king Ashoka,
Conquered India from top to toe.
He preached non–violence,
He was a king, even though.

> The great king Rajaraja Chola,
> Had the strongest navy in south Asia.
> With his weapons and strong warships,

His empire spread to Indonesia.

The great king Chandra Gupta,
Whose astronomer had powerful eyes.
He had the golden age,
Where Aryabhatta could scan the skies.

The great king Prithviraj,
Was a fierce Rajput warrior.
To aim an arrow at his enemy,
His blindness was not a barrier.

The great king Pratap,
At any cost, who would not bow.
He would crumble all his enemies,
And would slice them in a single blow.

The great queen Padmavati,
Bravely saved her women's pride,
The great fire consumed her,
She didn't, but her death died.

The great king Kumbha,
Made India's longest wall.
On seeing his valour,
His enemies would easily fall.

The great queen Laxmibai,
Women's greatest inspiration.
She roared like a lioness,
And always fought for her nation.

The great king Shivaji,
Born to break slavery's chain.

• 11 •

With his sharp sword and brain,
His enemies suffered severe pain.

They were born warriors,
Bloodshed was empire's base.
They had a wild passion,
Of facing enemies face – to – face.

6. WOH THE ABDUL KALAM.

Rameshwaram city me,
Janma ek aadmi aam.
Jisne scientific field me,
Banaya accha naam.

Jisne hamare India ko,
Diye parmanu salaam.
Jiski wajah se hamara desh,
Banaye ammunitions aur arm.
Woh the Abdul Kalam.

Jisne planning karke,
Dushman par lagayi lagaam.
Missiles acchi banakar,
Kari dushman ki neend haraam.

DRDO aur ISRO,
Jinka duniya mein hai accha naam.
Credit jaata hai uss insaan ko,
Jisne kiya yaha kaam.
Woh the Abdul Kalam.

Jiska dimaag tezz,
Aur nature ekdam calm.
Jisne aaj tak kabhi bhi,
Kisi ko nahi kiya harm.

Lectures dena, book likhna,
Hamesha jo karte the kaam.
Old age me bhi jo hamesha,
Nahi karte the aaraam.
Woh the Abdul Kalam.

Ban kar woh 11th president,
Desh ke bane humnam.
Desh ke rajneeti me aake,
Laaya pragati ka sangram.

Vision jinka time se aage,
Ideas jinki hui na naakaam.
Aisi thi woh personality,
Jinhe follow kare aawaam.
Woh the Abdul Kalam.

Lectures jinke hote atbhut,
Students par hota tha parinam.
Jaise ho wo koi magician,
Aur bolte ho koi charm.

Thoughts jinke hote inspiring,
Read kare log subah shaam.
Har samay jo kehte rehte,
Haarne par na karo vishram.
Woh the Abdul Kalam.

Jisne dekha ek sapna,
Bharat kare kuch aisa kaam.
21st century ho jaaye apni,
Aur duniya karti rahe pranam.

Hindu din, Christian city me,
Guzra jisne maana Islam.
Marte waqt bhi jis hasti ne,
De diya ekta ka paigam.
Woh the Abdul Kalam.

7. DESH SHARMINDA HAI. (Hindi version of THE SOIL CRIES).

Karam se imaandar, mann ke sacche,

Mehnat ka bojh uthate bacche,

Aaj yeh kehte hai,

> Chacha Nehru desh Sharminda hai,
>
> Baal majduri zinda hai.

Khoon se rangi har gulaab ki kali,

Har jalta sheher, har jalti galli,

Aaj yeh kehti hai,

> Gandhiji desh sharminda hai,
>
> Hinsa aaj zinda hai.

Desh ki sarhad par sainik ladte,

Dhushman ki goli khane par marte,

Aaj wo kehte hai,

> Netaji desh sharminda hai,
>
> Ghuspeth aaj zinda hai.

Ladkiyo ko shiksha se roka jaata,

Aur gharelu kaamo me jhoka jaata,

Aaj we kehti hai,

> Savitri desh sharminda hai,
>
> Stree shikshan par rok zinda hai.

Deen – dharm se desh hai bata,
Aur rajyo ke naam par jo hissa kata,
Aaj we kehte hai,

        Sardar Patel, desh sharminda hai,
          Batware aaj zinda hai.

Dahej – balatkar se desh hai haara,
Jinn ladkiyo ko garbh me hai maara,
Aaj we kehti hai,

        Rani Laxmibai, desh sharminda hai,
          Gharelu hinsa aaj zinda hai.

Jab raaj kare bhrashtrachaar,
Tab har gareeb jo bana shikar,
Aaj wo kehta hai,

        Chandrashekhar, desh sharminda hai,
          Lootmaar aaj zinda hai.

Jab aatankiyo ka ho satkar,
Aur Sarkar chalaye bekaar,
Tab desh ye kehta hai,

        Bhagat Singh, desh sharminda hai,
          Atanki hamle aaj zinda hai.

Jab apradhi karte hai aaj raaj,
Aur pehne nyaay ka jhoota taaj,
Tab har Bhartiya kehta hai,

        Mangal Pandey, desh sharminda hai,
          Gulaami aaj zinda hai. (2)

8. QUOTES FOR LIFE.

Old saying:
Work hard till your idols become your rivals.
New saying:
Work hard till your idols become your fans.
(Moral: the success which makes your good friends is far
better than the one which makes your enemies.)

The challenge is not to win the battle,
The challenge is to know
the power within us to win the battle.

The biggest mistakes we do
while working for our goals:

1. *I have time to start.*
2. *It's too late to start.*

The best teacher will
teach you self—study,
while the worst one
will force you to do the same.

The artist is the one who
creates himself the way he wants.

A good teacher teaches
the students to follow the teacher,

> while a bad student teaches the teacher
> to control the students.

*Fight in such a way that
even your snore is heard like a roar.*

> *The more you hold
> the tears in your eyes,
> the more your heart
> will turn into a stone.*

*By the seeds of war,
one can't grow a tree of peace.*

> *A thing that poses like a
> mountain in your path
> will give you the best
> iew once you climb it.*

*The sweat during your hard work
will give you the best fragrance.*

> *The level of your thinking
> shows the level of your work
> for the level you want to reach.*

*Your tombstone should read,
"LIVES FOREVER."*
(Moral: Live in such a way that
people will remember you always.)

> *Inside the huge heights,
> lies huge depths.*
> (Moral: every successful person (heights)
> has a deep story (depths).)

Too much comfort
will pork you in the end.

Every day can be a vacation
if you choose your hobby
as your profession.

Don't burn someone's road
just to light up their path.
(Moral: don't help someone so much that they
end up being helpless when left alone).

A single thread of love can cut even
the sharpest swords of hate.

Tears after failure are
medals of hard work.

Fire is common for all.
Some use it for burning others while
some use it to light up their own path.

You didn't forget to breathe today,
So why did you forget to live?

The best way to repair a noddy
brain is to make it struggle.

Be at the point where people
start plotting against you.

I am looking for myself within me.
(I am looking for the artist inside me
who will create the original me.)

Who am I? Ask this yourself
and let the world answer it.

Even a dog with allegiance
can attack a slaughterhouse.
(Moral: No matter how much the person is honest,
you should not blindly rely on him.)

Someone's speed can't lower your importance.
A windmill is slow,
but it is still much more powerful
then a speeding table fan.

Know the difference between
who wipes your tears
and who dries them.

"I can do it." Is said by someone
who knows everything
or knows nothing.
(Moral: If someone knows everything,
then he will be confident to do the task.
But sometimes he gets overconfident
to do the task without knowing it.)

I write because writing is the only world
in which I want to live.

You will be known by the
number of audiences you have.

Insults are the seeds of respect.

The right key is not enough
if you don't know the lock.
(Moral: Sometimes, we are having the solution.
But because of not knowing the problem properly,

we fail to use the solution wisely.)

> The one who inspects is disturbed,
> while the one who introspects is peaceful.

A school teaches a good deed
a thousand times
and it is done just once.
A religious place teaches a good deed
just once
and it is done thousand times.

> The day you start hating yourself
> is the day you realize that
> you are full of mistakes.
> And the day you start loving yourself
> is the day you realize
> you can overcome your mistakes.

If you are ruling on yourself,
then you need not conquer
the whole world.

> The best photographer
> will explain the content without words.
> The best writer
> will explain the content without images.

The easier the job,
the higher the competition.
The tough the job,
the higher the monopoly.

> Don't compete with the ones

who are winning on another field.